ACTIVE
CITIZENSHIP
TODAY

Standing Up
to Hate Speech

Alison Morretta

Cavendish
Square

New York

Published in 2018 by Cavendish Square Publishing, LLC
243 5th Avenue, Suite 136, New York, NY 10016

Copyright © 2018 by Cavendish Square Publishing, LLC

First Edition

Library of Congress Cataloging-in-Publication Data

Names: Morretta, Alison, author.
Title: Standing Up to hate speech / Alison Morretta.
Description: New York : Cavendish Square Publishing, 2018 | Series: Active citizenship today | Includes bibliographical references and index. | Audience: Grades 2-6.
Identifiers: LCCN 2017023199 (print) | LCCN 2017035367 (ebook) |
ISBN 9781502629302 (library bound) | ISBN 9781502629289 (pbk.) |
ISBN 9781502629296 (6 pack) | ISBN 9781502629319 (E-book)
Subjects: LCSH: Hate speech--Juvenile literature. |
Communication--Psychological aspects--Juvenile literature.
Classification: LCC HM1166 (ebook) | LCC HM1166 .M67 2018 (print) |
DDC 302.2/2--dc23
LC record available at https://lccn.loc.gov/2017023199

Editorial Director: David McNamara
Editor: Fletcher Doyle
Copy Editor: Nathan Heidelberger
Associate Art Director: Amy Greenan
Designer: Joe Parenteau
Production Coordinator: Karol Szymczuk
Photo Research: J8 Media

The photographs in this book are used by permission and through the courtesy of: Cover Alina555/E+/Getty Images; p. 4 Donald Iain Smith/Blend Images/Getty Images; p. 6 Peter Dazeley/Photographer's Choice/Getty Images; p. 7 Richard Tsong-Taatarii/ The Star Tribune/AP Photo; p. 8 (top right) wavebreakmedia/Shutterstock.com; p. 8 (bottom left) Pete Souza/The White House; p. 9 SolStock/iStock; p. 10 Bettmann/Getty Images; p. 11 Jupiterimages/Creatas Images/Thinkstock; p. 12 XiXinXing/ iStock; p. 14, 16 Blend Images – KidStock/Brand X Pictures/Getty Images; p. 15 Image Source/Getty Images; p. 19 Gideon Mendel/Corbis Documentary/Getty Images; p. 20 monkeybusinessimages/iStock; p. 22 asiseeit/iStock; p. 24 Eri Morita/Taxi Japan/Getty Images; p. 25 Boogich/iStock; p. 26 Monica Schipper/Getty Images for the New York Women's Foundation.

Printed in the United States of America

CONTENTS

Defining
Hate Speech

At a Georgia middle school, a Sikh boy was called "terrorist." Students on his bus made fun of his **turban**. Sikhs wear turbans as a sign of their religion. He stood up for himself. He told the other students that they were being racist. His bullies were punished. This does not always

Opposite: In this Sikh family portrait, the women are wearing traditional clothing. The men are wearing turbans.

happen. Some victims of **hate speech** are too scared to stand up to bullies. Children and adults need others to help them and support them. That is why it is important to know what hate speech is. It is good to know how it hurts people.

Being the victim of cyberbullying is upsetting.

What Is Hate Speech?

Hate speech is a form of bullying. It is discrimination based on a person's identity. It includes **slurs**. These are words used to make someone feel bad. Slurs **target** race. They target religion. Some slurs insult girls. Hate speech is often posted on social media. Writing slurs or hate symbols on buildings is considered a hate crime. It is illegal.

Temple Israel in Minnesota was vandalized during Passover in 2013.

Hate speech is a form of **prejudice**. People who are prejudiced **judge** others without knowing them. They have a **bias** against a group. Bias is favoring one person over another. They make decisions based on **stereotypes**. A stereotype is something believed about all people in a group. Stereotypes can seem positive but still hurt people. Saying a person is good at sports or good at math because they are part of a group can hurt them.

Sometimes people are bullied because of their gender.

How Hate Speech Hurts

People can use hate speech without hating someone. Often it comes from not knowing people. When you spend time with people, you get to know them. You learn

President Obama signs the Hate Crimes Prevention Act into law.

which words hurt them. Words cause emotional pain. Punching someone causes physical pain. Violence can scare those who see it.

Bullying hurts victims and those who see it. Bullying can make everyone around feel afraid.

Victims of hate speech often feel sad and afraid. They don't want to go to school. They have a hard time listening in class. This can lead to

RUBY BRIDGES

Ruby Bridges started first grade in 1960. She is African American. She was the first black child to go to an all-white elementary school in the South. Crowds outside the school threatened Ruby. They shouted slurs at her. School was hard for Ruby. White parents would not let their children go to the school. Ruby was brave. She overcame the racism. Today she runs her own foundation and fights for equality.

Victims of bullying often feel lonely at school. This can make them want to hurt themselves.

bad grades. They may feel lonely. They may feel bad about themselves. They would rather be like someone else. Words can make people so sad that they want to harm themselves. Someone may get so angry that they want to hurt other people.

Fighting Hate Speech

How should you treat people? The way you want them to treat you. You wouldn't want to be called names because of something you can't change. You wouldn't want to be judged on your skin color. You can't change where your family comes from.

Opposite: A family celebrates Chinese New Year outside of their store.

Spending time with someone one-on-one can break down stereotypes.

Be an Ally

What do you do when someone else is called names? What if people around you are saying offensive things to somebody? What if they are your friends? You should still speak up against prejudice. Stand up for people who are being treated unfairly. This is called being an **ally**. It helps victims of hate speech feel less alone.

If you don't feel safe speaking up, that is OK. The person using hate speech may be an adult you don't know. But don't join the crowd when it treats someone badly. Think about how the person being attacked must feel. Don't be pressured into saying bad things. You like being part of a crowd. However, don't say mean things to fit in. Don't say them because others in the crowd are doing it.

Comforting someone who has been bullied can make that person feel less alone.

If you have been a victim of hate speech, tell an adult. Never be afraid to ask for help. Let someone know if you have heard something offensive. If you see or hear something about someone at school, tell your teacher.

How to Fight Hate Speech

Here are a few things to do when you hear hate speech:

✓ **Politely ask the speaker to stop.** The speaker may not realize that what he or

A boy in a wheelchair has an ally working with him in class.

she is saying is hurtful. Avoid personal attacks when you ask someone to stop.

✓ **Ask the speaker a question.** You can say something like, "What do you mean by that?" or "Why do you think that is funny?" People don't often think about their prejudices. Simple questions may make a person stop and think.

✓ **Don't join in.** Sometimes people, especially bullies, do things for attention. They do something because they think it's cool. By not joining in, you can show them that it's not cool.

✓ **Help the victim get away.** Sometimes a bully just won't stop. The best thing you can do is to be an ally to the victim. Eat lunch with them. Play with them at recess. Walk with them to class. Help the victim feel less alone.

✓ **Tell the victim it's not their fault.** Hate speech victims may feel they deserve the abuse. It's right to tell them that they did nothing wrong.

MOST COMMON TYPES OF HATE SPEECH

Ethnicity: 54 percent

Nationality: 25 percent

Social Class: 7 percent

Religion: 6 percent

Sexual Orientation: 3 percent

Gender: 3 percent

Disability: 2 percent

Teachers are trained to resolve problems with bullying.

✓ **Tell an adult.** There are situations you can't fix. Your teachers and parents are there to help you. Hate speech attacks usually happen when adults are not around. You have to let someone know what has happened. Teachers are trained to deal with these problems. They know how to enforce the rules.

3

Joining the Fight

To be a good citizen, try to learn about other people. Enjoy the **diversity** of our world. Diversity makes the world fun. There is always something new to learn. If every place and everybody were the same, life would be boring.

Opposite: Diversity is fun and something to enjoy.

The library is a great place to learn about different people and cultures.

Get Educated

It's normal to be curious about the things we see and hear. It is natural to wonder about people who are different. They may look different. They may speak another language. They may have an accent. They may wear different clothes. These things don't tell you about the person. Do not assume the person is bad or strange. Don't judge others based on how they look. It is a form of prejudice. Practice **tolerance**. This means accepting things that are different. It doesn't mean accepting things that are bad. Don't tolerate hate speech. Get to know the person. You probably will find that you have things in common.

Combat prejudice by educating yourself. Start at your school or public library. Ask a librarian to help you find books and videos. Study other countries and their cultures. Learn about different religions. Ask about anything you want to know. Fight hate with learning. Share what you learn with others.

Get Organized

Is there a multicultural club at your school? If not, start one. It's a way to get different kinds of people together. Invite everybody. Everyone can learn about each other. What games do you each play? What music do you each like? That can break down stereotypes. You can also join organized activities outside of school. Ask your parents to help you find events in your town or city that celebrate others.

A Japanese family celebrates a traditional Buddhist festival.

Try Something New

Everyone has routines. We eat the same food. We watch the same television shows. We listen to the same kind of music. To experience anything new, we have to break these habits. It can take some effort. There is a whole world out there of new things to try. It will be worth the energy to find them. Go to an **ethnic** festival. Watch a foreign movie. Listen to music from a different country.

Standing Up to Hate Speech

Eat a new kind of food. You might like it or you might not. It's OK if you don't. Either way, you learn to respect other cultures.

Trying foods from another culture is a delicious way to celebrate diversity.

Book Report

Read a book about a kid your age who is different than you. The kid can be fictional or a real-life person. Maybe they have a different skin color. Maybe they need a wheelchair. They could practice a different religion or live in a different country. After you've finished, make two lists. The first lists the ways the person is the same as you. The second lists the ways they are different. Look at the second list. Place a check mark next to differences that are part of the person's identity. Those are the things targeted by hate speech.

MARLEY DIAS

Marley Dias loves to read. She was upset that no books had people who looked like she does. At eleven years old, she started #1000blackgirlbooks. She wanted to find one thousand books with a black girl as the main character. Her work led to a book deal. It gave her the chance to write her own book. She wrote about volunteering to help others. She also wrote about including everybody in activities.

Glossary

ally Someone who speaks up for or comforts someone else.

bias Prejudice for or against a person or group. It is usually negative.

diversity The variety of human beings and cultures.

ethnic Describing a large group of people who share racial, cultural, religious, and language backgrounds.

hate speech Words that attack or threaten groups of people.

judge To form a bad opinion
about a person or action.

prejudice An idea formed about
people without knowing about them.

slur A hurtful and harmful word or phrase
about another person or group.

stereotype A simple image or idea
about every person in a group.

target Pick someone from a
group as the aim of an attack.

tolerance Accepting beliefs or
practices different than yours.

turban A long cloth wrapped around the head.

Find Out More

Books

Berry, Joy. *Every Kid's Guide to Overcoming Prejudice and Discrimination*. Wheaton, IL: Watkins Publishing House, 2013.

Lester, Julius. *Let's Talk About Race*. New York: Amistad Press, 2008.

Tonatiuh, Duncan. *Separate Is Never Equal: Sylvia Mendez and Her Family's Fight for Desegregation*. New York: Harry N. Abrams, 2014.

Websites

Do Something

https://www.dosomething.org/us

Kids can join with others to do something good.

Kids Against Bullying

http://www.pacerkidsagainstbullying.org/kab

Read about bullying and ways to stop it.

McGruff the Crime Dog: Advice

http://www.mcgruff.org/#/Advice

This site has games, videos, and advice for kids on subjects such as bullying.

Index

About the Author

Alison Morretta holds a bachelor of arts in English and creative writing from Kenyon College in Gambier, Ohio, where she studied literature and American history. She has written many nonfiction titles for students on subjects such as American literature, colonial America, the abolitionist movement, the civil rights era, and internet safety. She lives in New York with her loving husband, Bart, and their corgi, Cassie.